SCOTLAND'S INDEPENDENT COACH OPERATORS

DAVID DEVOY

AMBERLEY

First published 2018

Amberley Publishing
The Hill, Stroud
Gloucestershire, GL5 4EP

www.amberley-books.com

Copyright © David Devoy, 2018

The right of David Devoy to be identified as
the Author of this work has been asserted in
accordance with the Copyrights, Designs and
Patents Act 1988.

ISBN 978 1 4456 7456 8 (print)
ISBN 978 1 4456 7457 5 (ebook)

British Library Cataloguing in Publication Data.
A catalogue record for this book is available from
the British Library.

Origination by Amberley Publishing.
Printed in the UK.

Introduction

Around 70 per cent of Scotland's population live in the Central Lowlands—a region stretching in a northeast–southwest orientation between the major cities of Edinburgh and Glasgow, and including the major settlements of Paisley, Stirling, Falkirk, Perth and Dundee, so it comes as no surprise to find more bus and coach operators in these areas.

Coaching in Scotland is divided into various categories: private hires, works and school contracts, excursions, express services and tours and holidays. Some of these are more seasonal than others, but operators must keep the wheels turning throughout the year to make a profit. Vehicles are specified for the jobs they are used on; sometimes a high seating capacity is required, or a toilet, or a smaller vehicle or even a double-decker. Some firms always buy new whereas others find the second-hand market suits their budgets.

Major operators could order vehicles directly from the manufacturers, but smaller operators had to use specialised dealers. The major manufacturers encouraged this as they could achieve higher-volume standardised production runs by limiting the available options. It often suited operators as they could trade in their old vehicles against a new purchase. By the early 1970s Scotland had three coach dealers. E. & N. Sanderson began as an operator, but sold out in the early 1920s to concentrate on selling commercial vehicles. He and his brother formed Millburn Motors in the late 1920s, based at Millburn Street in Glasgow. The firm also had premises in Preston, allowing many ex-Leyland demonstrators to be purchased over the years. The firm also had a financial interest in Lowland Motorways of Glasgow and Hutchison's of Overtown. Two directors, namely Ernest Sanderson and Alex Norris, left in 1971 to form S&N Motors, based in Colston Road in Glasgow. This firm changed hands in 1976 when Dorada Holdings purchased the share capital for £290,000, but the dealership only lasted for another couple of years. SMT Sales and Service Ltd were also based in the city at Finnieston, and were a remnant of the Scottish Motor Traction Group, which had owned many of the bus companies in Scotland. The bus companies were sold to the state in 1948, but the Vauxhall car and Bedford coach dealerships remained in private hands.

Glasgow-based bus and coach dealer Millburn Motors had close links to the Scottish Bus Group and were able to sell surplus vehicles to operators in England through their Preston branch, but it was rare that a Scottish operator could buy any as there was a clause in the contract forbidding their use in Scotland. The odd exception could be made: for example if a Bus Group vehicle was in a collision with a private operator's vehicle, then an ex-SBG vehicle could be used to cover the cost of any damage caused. Millburn held the franchise for the British Leyland and Ford marques, while S&N Motors were Ford dealers but later added Volvo to their portfolio, and SMT sold the Bedford range. All held stocks of second-hand vehicles. Glasgow was also home to Blythswood Motors, who held second-hand stock. The dealers would order a batch of vehicles for stock, which were often built to a variety of specifications with different bodies. The business was seasonal as most operators would want new coaches delivered in time for the start of the new coaching season, around April. In 1967 there were 683 Scottish bus and coach operators, and they owned 9,365 vehicles between them.

The introduction of Volvo chassis in 1972 shook the market up. This was an expensive premium product, but for companies like Park's of Hamilton this was the way ahead. Douglas Park was only twenty-two years old and had his own ideas, and switched to the heavyweight Volvo B58 as the company was running more and more long-distance private hires and excursions throughout Britain; soon enough, the black coaches became a well-known trademark. On the coachbuilding front Van Hool sold their first Volvo B58s in 1975 and this proved to be a winning combination.

A new addition to the dealers came in 1976, when the Moseley Group opened a showroom in Coatbridge, while Kirkby opened premises in Carluke, later moving to Hillington. They were later joined by Tony Andrews of Stair (backed by the Anderson family who owned Hutchison's of Overtown) and Cotter's Sales & Service, which was based in Alexandra Parade in Glasgow (later renamed as Caledonia) and supplied Volvo and Ford chassis, and Van Hool coachwork. Scania dealer Reliable Vehicles were based at Newbridge on the outskirts of Edinburgh. Green's of Kirkintilloch later supplied second-hand vehicles through their Regal Coaches dealership based in their home town. Drew Wilson (of the Wilson's family who ran in Carnwath) later joined the fray with a dealership based at Carluke. Roselare Coach Sales operated out of a corner of Graham's Bus Services' Hawkhead premises briefly too. This firm was set up by coach operator John Jeffs and Alan Wilson, and was named after the Belgian town where Jonckheere built their coaches. The coach dealers would hold trade shows at their own premises every two years to coincide with the Scottish Motor Show, held at the Kelvin Hall in Glasgow biennially and hosted by the Scottish Motor Traders Association. Here the industry would show off all the latest models and services available to operators. This was where the 'small operator' could see models that he could not realistically afford to buy, but might aspire to in a few years' time once they hit the second-hand market. It kept operators in touch with developments in the industry, and was often a social occasion for meeting other operators during a day off.

Alongside the official dealer network there were, and still are, some 'operator-dealers' who often buy new vehicles and sell them on after a season or two. Names that come to mind are Wallace Arnold, Shearings, Hutchison's and Rennie's, etc. Smaller operators often let their larger neighbours try out new models and fix any weaknesses or defects in their design before committing to a purchase. Most operators tend to stick with well-known chassis and body combinations as a better price will always be obtained for a mainstream product than for obscure niche products, which can be a nightmare when trying to obtain spare parts in later life. Sadly, too many firms nowadays use a white or silver base colour with a few vinyls to break up the monotony. It must be said that it is easier to sell a plain-coloured coach on the second-hand market, but sadly a lot of the individuality has been lost in the process. Some of the colour schemes used in the past were almost a work of art, and were a source of great pride for their owners.

Many operators began in the 1920s and the strongest expanded and eliminated weaker firms. Many businesses were small-scale family owned and would be passed through the generations. There was often a great pride taken in the presentation of these small fleets, and many companies had their own colour schemes. Sometimes this would be original, or the colour a dealer may have chosen for a stock vehicle, or sometimes the livery on a second-hand coach would be adopted for the whole fleet. Signwriting was normally applied on the exterior as the coach was the greatest advert for potential customers. As the years passed transfers were applied and then vinyl took over. Some smaller firms would use names on their vehicles to distinguish them, such as *Southern Rose*, *Scottish Ambassador* and *Janice*, while Garelochhead Coach Services named their fleet after the Scottish lochs.

Licences were needed for everything, whether it was a new tour, picking up points or express services. Other firms in the area would normally object to safeguard their own businesses, as could British Rail. Sometimes a maximum number of coaches that could be used was specified. The traffic commissioners' decision was final. It must be said that this system stifled innovation but it all changed after the Traffic Act 1980 deregulated the market. Express coach services over 50 km were deregulated, and this led to a flurry of new coach services and operators. This competition led to an increase in standards and favoured operators of heavyweight chassis. The Act also gave coach operators more freedom to operate longer distance and even Continental holidays. Gross weight became an issue as double glazing, reclining seats, toilets and galley all added weight. Integral vehicles began to be accepted as European manufacturers launched new products in the UK. An answer to the weight problem led to coaches being fitted with a trailing axle fitted behind the rear axle. Vehicles could be built to a length of 15 metres and still comply with turning-circle regulations as the rear wheels could be turned when steering.

At one time it was common for coaches to be delicenced over the lean winter months, as there was not enough work to keep the whole fleet occupied. Likewise, drivers were often employed on a seasonal basis. The same went for the coachbuilders, who were busy in the winter building orders for the following season, but were quiet in the summer. Many of these were based in seaside towns where other summer work was readily available for the staff. Many coach companies faced competition from their nationalised cousins, but from around the 1970s onwards staff shortages and the purchase of unsuitable dual-purpose vehicles helped the independents to thrive.

Most companies tended to buy cheaper lightweight chassis, but a few always purchased heavyweights. Unlike buses, the coach industry is more prone to changing fashion and vehicles could be seen as old-fashioned as people's perceptions changed. An example of this could be seen in the amount of chrome bright-work in use declining over the years. The car industry also influenced coach design over the years. The expanding motorway network also led to a demand for more powerful vehicles as the distance travelled in a day increased. Many operators stuck with the same dealers year in year out as a rapport was built up. From time to time operators have had sound chassis with out-of-date bodywork, or victims of accidents re-bodied to produce almost new-looking coaches. The use of Irish and cherished registration plates has become popular over the years to disguise the age of a vehicle, and probably began when travel agencies began to impose age limits on the coaches they hired in. Sometimes holiday companies want the coaches to bear their own in-house liveries with their brand names rather than the operator's. Firms that come to mind are Caledonian Travel and David Urquhart Tours, but there are others. The operators normally get paid a premium for doing this, and are usually guaranteed a minimum amount of work for the year.

Over the years many firms have fallen by the wayside for various reasons. Sometimes there was no successor, or family members sought an easier life elsewhere. Contracts could be lost, leaving a business unprofitable, or premises might need to be replaced over time, especially as the length of coaches increased. The fleet itself needs constant investment to remain modern. Passenger expectations have risen over the years and operators have had to keep pace with this. The coaches themselves were getting longer and higher to provide more luggage space, and air suspension became the norm. Engine exhaust emissions became tougher and engine management systems required the use of computer diagnostics. Speed limiters had to be fitted, seatbelts became mandatory for school contracts, meaning older coaches had to be retro-fitted, although they are fitted as standard on new vehicles nowadays. From 1 January 2008 express coaches were banned from using the third lane of motorways by Section 4 of the Motorways Traffic Act.

The use of hire-purchase has changed the market drastically over the years as credit has become easier to obtain. Dealers will even rent out coaches for a season nowadays, but this wasn't always the case. At one time a company would have to keep a coach throughout its life to ensure a profit from their investment. Regulations have been tightened up over the years in regard to drivers' hours, rest days, tachographs and speed limiters. The industry operates 24/7 and drivers' hours can be long. Rail replacement work has increased over the years when railway lines are closed for maintenance work and many companies chase this work as it often occurs during the winter and over bank holidays when schools are closed, freeing up drivers.

My own involvement in the industry started when I was about twelve years of age. A school friend and I got to know our local coach operator, Travelmac Coaches, owned by a neighbour called Tommy MacDonald. We used to help clean the coaches after school and at the weekends. We sold tickets for mystery tours during the school holidays and handled telephone enquiries. We could travel on these excursions for free, and were taken to the dealers for spare parts or to look at new coaches when the opportunity arose. Trade magazines were delivered to the company and kept us up to date with happenings in the industry, who was selling what and who had new coaches to look out for. They were all we had apart from word of mouth as there was no Internet in those days. It seems that everything is available now at the touch of a button, with information and pictures appearing almost instantaneously, but we have lost the genuine air of excitement of seeing something we did not even know about.

We had both intended to enter the industry as drivers when we were old enough and had even talked about starting our own company in the future. My life took another turn, however, after I left school to start an apprenticeship as a marine pipework engineer. Our old employer passed away and we went our separate ways. In 1988 I did consider becoming an operator, and even priced a few coaches. I nearly purchased a Volvo from Henderson's of Carstairs, but got cold feet in the end. Eventually I did get my licence, but have always driven service buses. I have always kept abreast of happenings in the industry and have been taking photographs ever since. Many of the companies featured in this book are no longer in business, so it is nice to record some of them in print.

I dedicate this book to my wife, Susan Devoy (1960–2017), for her encouragement in whatever I was doing. I'd like to thank my daughter Samantha for her help in proof reading. I'd also like to thank my many friends in the industry for allowing me to photograph their fleets over my lifetime, sometimes even washing coaches especially for my visit.

BSD 560C was an AEC Reliance 2U3RA/Duple (Northern) Alpine Continental C51F that was purchased new by Dodd's of Troon in May 1965. It was on a visit to Paris when snapped at Notre Dame. The chassis was still sound by 1980, but the coachwork was getting dated, so it was decided to rebody it with a new Willowbrook 003 body.

LGG 762E was an AEC Reliance 2U3RA/Alexander Y Type C49F that was delivered new to the Scottish Co-operative Wholesale Society, Glasgow, for their Majestic Coaches fleet in May 1967. It passed to Altincham Coachways of West Timperley and Guiseley Tours of Yeadon before reaching Irvine's of Law in April 1975, and was captured passing through Motherwell.

Captured a long way from home while visiting the beautiful city of Chester, we find DGG 7K. It was a Leyland Leopard PSU3B/4R/Plaxton Elite C51F that was purchased new in 1973, and is still looking remarkably smart six years later. Alexander Doig had begun operating buses in 1909 and ran services from Greenock in the 1920s. In July 1931 his three services were sold to Greenock Motor Services and the fleet refocused on coaches.

MGB 277E was a Leyland Leopard PSU3/3R/Plaxton Panorama C47F that was purchased new by Cotter's Tours of Glasgow in June 1967. Bernard Cotter began operating coaches in 1930 and found a niche in the market by offering tours for religious pilgrims to Lourdes and Rome. The company also held the prestigious contract to transport Glasgow Celtic F.C.

VGG 722R was a Bedford YMT/Plaxton Supreme C53F that was purchased new by Southern Coaches of Barrhead in May 1977. Operations began in 1960, based at Lochlibo Garage in Barrhead. The fleet was easily recognised as the registration numbers contained the letters 'SOU' in various combinations. Sadly, it closed down in April 2018.

KSM 801P was a Ford R1114/Duple Dominant C49F that was purchased new by Gibson's of Moffat in April 1976, and was exhibited at the Blackpool Coach Rally on collection from the Duple Coachbuilding factory in the town. It would run until October 1987 before being cannibalised for spares. Gibson's ran from 1922 until the business closed down in 2007.

LCS 782P was an AEC Reliance 6U3ZR/Plaxton Elite Express C53F that was purchased new by Clyde Coast co-operative member McGregor of Saltcoats in November 1975. It replaced SXD 246L, a 1973 Ford that was sold to Donnachie of Crosshill. LCS, however, remained in the fleet until December 1982, when it passed to Mackay of Newtongrange before joining Roy Lonie of Loanhead.

DCU 19 was a Bedford SB1/Duple C41F that was delivered new to Hall Bros of South Shields in May 1960. On disposal it passed to Weir's Tours of Bowling, then joined Smith's of Easdale in 1967. It was retained until mechanical failure led to its withdrawal shortly before the business was sold to MacColl of Benderloch on 15 May 1972.

KGA 316N was a Bristol LHS6L/Plaxton Supreme C33F that was purchased new by Duncan Stewart of Dalmuir in May, and it was Scotland's first LHS. It later worked for Jones of Macclesfield and Cross Gates Coaches. CGE 16S was a similar example, purchased in June 1978. After the death of the founder, the company became a co-operative for a spell before being renamed as McColl's Coaches.

TAG 770J was a Bedford SB5/Duple C41F that was delivered new to Dodd's of Troon in May 1971, and ran until May 1978. James Dodd founded his business in 1910 with bus services, coach tours, vehicle maintenance, a Ford car dealership and televison/video shops added. The coach fleet was separated in 1948 when the threat of nationalisation was very real, and remains in business to the present day, but is nowadays garaged in Ayr.

A fine pair of 1975 deliveries to Hutchison's of Overtown built on AEC Reliance chassis. HHS 386N had a Duple Dominant body, was a diverted order, and was delivered in this non-standard livery. JGE 387N had a Plaxton Elite III body. Isaac Hutchison set up in business in 1918, but retired in 1959. The firm was purchased by Ernest Sanderson, the Millburn Motors director, and local haulage-operator Sam Anderson. Full control passed to the Anderson family, who continued to run it until 2007.

PSD 521R was a Leyland Leopard PSU5A/4R/Plaxton Supreme C57F that was purchased new by Jock Shennan of Drongan in January 1977. It later passed to Yorkshire operator Joseph Wood of Mirfield. The turnover of used vehicles was relentless, with many lasting only a matter of months, but the business eventually collapsed.

LDS 381V was a Leyland Leopard PSU3E/4R/Plaxton Supreme C51F that was purchased new by Garelochhead Coach Services in September 1979. All coaches carried the name of a Scottish loch, and this one was *Loch Morlich*. Sadly, its stay would be brief, as the company ceased operations in 1980, which was thought to have been caused by a massive loss of MOD contracts. This coach later ran for De-Luxe of Mancetter.

4324 UA, an AEC Reliance 2MU3RA/Duple Britannia C41F that was purchased new by Wallace Arnold Tours of Leeds in 1959. It passed to Cosgrove of Dundee as their fleet number 24 in 1968 and ran until the mid-1970s. The Duple Britannia was based on the Elizabethan range, but with vertical pillars, and was introduced in 1955.

SSB 817L was a Ford R226/Willowbrook Expressway 002 C53F that was purchased new by Cowal Motors of Dunoon in April 1973. The Willowbrook coachbuilding business was acquired by Duple in 1958, although it continued to operate under its own name. It became independent once again in 1971 and the Expressway was intended to break into the coach market.

GSU 717N was a Volvo B58-56/Plaxton Elite Express C51F that was delivered new to Irvine's of Salsburgh for their Golden Eagle fleet in January 1975. It later ran for Robb's of Brechin and was re-registered as UES 572. It moved to Fraser of Duncanton, then to Norries of New Deer in 1992, and passed to Stagecoach Bluebird with the business in early 1994. It was disposed of to Rennie's of Dunfermline in August 1994.

HSG 723N was a Bedford YRT/Plaxton Elite C53F that was purchased new by Silver Fox Coaches of Edinburgh in February 1975. On disposal in 1977 it passed to Austin's of Earlston. It then moved to Munro's of Jedburgh and is seen in Hawick on a hire by Jedburgh Thistle F.C. The company was founded in the mid-1960s by Jimmy Munro, who expanded his hire car business to include coach operations. Sadly, Munro's ceased trading at midnight on 3 July 2013.

UHS 359R was a Ford R1114/Duple Dominant C53F that was purchased new by Allander Travel of Milngavie in April 1977, seen at the Blackpool Coach Rally when new. The company was started by Jimmy Wilson in 1960 and is still in business. The firm takes its name from an area of Milngavie. In addition to the front-line coaches, a contract fleet is also operated.

LVD 809L was a Bedford YRT/Duple Dominant C53F that was delivered new to Park's of Hamilton in April 1973. Park's of Hamilton can trace its roots back to 1949, when Park's Thistle Coaches, originally based in Strathaven, started, but the present company only dates from 1971, when the company was reconstituted. LVD 809L later worked for Boyden International and Midway of Eccles, later being re-registered as HIL 2574.

TSY 136M was a Leyland Leopard PSU5/4RT/Caetano Cascais II C57F that was purchased new by Black's of Gorebridge in March 1974. It subsequently moved to Ambassador of Edinburgh before purchase by John Boyce. It was working on rail replacement services at Paisley Gilmour Street. John was the fleet engineer for Duncan Stewart Coaches, but ran a couple of his own coaches at the same time. It was sold to Islay Coaches in October 1986 and they ran it until the early 1990s.

B494 UNB was a Leyland Tiger TRCTL11/3RZ/Plaxton Paramount 3500 C53F that was new as Shearings of Altrincham fleet number 494 in March 1985. It passed to Earnside Coaches of Glenfarg in 1991, and was snapped in Glasgow. The livery was inspired by York Pullman after a second-hand coach was purchased, although the proportions have been altered over the years. The business can trace its roots back to 1968.

West Coast Motors are one of Scotland's largest independents nowadays, but that wasn't always the case. A couple of coaches from earlier days are recalled here. PUJ 782 was a Leyland Tiger Cub PSUC1/2/Burlingham Seagull C41F new to Whittle of Highley in January 1958, while 5650 PT was a Bedford SB1/Yeates B44F that was purchased new by Bond Bros of Willington in June 1961. The founding of the company dates back to 1923 when Jack Craig commenced a bus operation in Campbeltown.

TGD 991R was a beautiful Volvo B58-56/Plaxton Viewmaster C53F that was purchased new in March 1977. These vehicles took coach design in Britain to new levels and were certainly eye-catching. It would later pass to Telling's Coaches and Tricolour Coaches. The Plaxton Viewmaster was a taller version of the Supreme III or IV, with the height increased by approximately 10 inches, and a total of 211 were built.

DYS 558T was a Leyland Leopard PSU5C/4R/Plaxton Supreme C57Ft that was purchased new by Gold Circle of Airdrie in August 1978. It passed to Simpson's of Rosehearty, and is seen at Ullapool Harbour. Good business was obtained from the fishing boats by taking the crews home to all over the UK in between voyages. The coach would later pass to Irvine's of Law for further service.

UGB 18R was an AEC Reliance 6U3ZR/Duple Dominant II C51F that was delivered new to Hutchison's of Overtown in April 1977, and is seen after collection at the Blackpool Coach Rally. It passed to George Milligan of Mauchline in January 1983, then Fred Ayres of Dalkeith in December 1986, and then moved to Clark's of Banchory, where it was re-registered as RZ7 430 and remained long enough to serve JW Coaches of Banchory when they purchased the business in 1992.

3196 DD was a Van Hool Astron T818 CH60Ft that was purchased new in June 1983 for use on 'Fast Class' express services ran by Newton's of Dingwall, Allander Travel and Dunnet's of Keiss, linking Glasgow/Edinburgh to Inverness/Wick/Thurso and Ullapool. It was a high-class operation, providing snacks, drinks and videos, etc. At the time the Scottish Bus Group were running Leyland Leopards and Tigers, which just could not compete, so there was great relief when Newton's sold out in December 1985. The location was St Andrew Square in Edinburgh.

Cotter's Coachline was set up as a separate company to operate express services between Scotland and London using a fleet of eight Volvo B10Ms fitted with forty-seat Van Hool Alizee bodies featuring a galley. Hostesses served hot drinks and blankets were provided on the night journeys. The company had its own coach station in Glasgow. This operation was sold to Stagecoach of Perth, and continued for a spell using the same vehicles. UHV 59 was destroyed in a fire and was replaced by a Neoplan in standard Stagecoach livery, but with the fleet names amended to 'Coachline'.

XNU 463F was a Leyland Leopard PSU4/3R/Duple (Northern) Commander C43F that was purchased new by Mycock of Monyash in July 1968. On disposal in January 1970 it joined Rennie's of Dunfermline before reaching Garnock Valley in 1973. It passed with the business to Paterson's in 1975, and was still in GV livery in April 1977. Garnock Valley was set up in 1953 to acquire the Kilbirnie and Beith operations of Northern Ayrshire Coaches, which was a subsidiary of Northern Roadways of Glasgow.

SVD 204M was a Leyland Leopard PSU3B/4R/Duple Dominant Express C53F that was delivered new to Irvine's of Law on 24 April 1974. This fine-looking coach featured a six-speed gearbox. It later passed to Brabyn's Coaches of Marple. Irvine's of Law was formed in 1959, with Law Bus & Coach added later on as a separate company under the name of Margaret Walker. Sadly, the business collapsed in 2012.

9914 UG was an AEC Reliance 2MU3RA/Plaxton Panorama C41C that was purchased new by Wallace Arnold Tours of Leeds in April 1961. It passed to Elizabeth Yule of Pitlochry and was seen passing Loch Tummel in Perthshire. The firm also run taxis and local bus services. Wallace Arnold often kept the second-hand market afloat as they changed their fleet every few years and released modern coaches to other fleets.

UNY 878G was a Ford R226/Duple Viceroy C53F that was delivered new to Bebb's of Llantwit Fardre in January 1969. It passed to Stanley MacKay of Portobello before reaching Wilson's of Carnwath. The Wilson family began operating buses in the 1920s, and have bought out several other operators over the years, the largest being Nationwide Coaches of Lanark in 1990.

TVU 950 was a Bedford SBG/Duple Vega C41F that was purchased new by North Manchester Coaches of Moston in April 1957. It passed to Dunnet's of Keiss, and was captured at their depot. The commercial services passed to Highland Bus & Coach in 1992, leaving behind a small coach business, which later passed to Sutherland of Wick.

WSC 33R was a Bedford YMT/Plaxton Supreme C53F that was delivered new to Silver Fox Coaches of Edinburgh in April 1977. There was no connection between the Silver Fox companies of Glasgow and Edinburgh. The Edinburgh firm adopted the fleet name when sub-contracted after a large contract was won by the Glasgow firm from Thomson Holidays to serve both Glasgow and Edinburgh airports. The customer demanded that all coaches used carried the same fleet names.

TAG 516M was a Volvo B58-56/Duple Dominant C53F that was purchased new by Paterson's of Dalry in June 1974 and it would serve in the fleet until 1986. This view as delivered in the 'continental stripes' colour scheme, which was popular at the time. Paterson's were established in 1948 and ran until operations ceased in February 2006.

GDU 66L was a UTIC C53F that was purchased new by Bonas of Coventry, trading as Supreme Coaches, in 1972. Portuguese manufacturer UTIC is well known for building vehicles based on AEC running units over a considerable period of years, continuing to do so even after the 1979 closure of Southall works. A small batch of nine UTIC U2043 integrals were imported into the UK by Loughborough dealer Moseley's. The first was registered in August 1971 and was purchased by L. F. Bowen of Birmingham. Bowen's only kept it for two months but then surprisingly purchased two others in 1974, which had previously been operated by Bonas of Coventry.

EUS 10C was an AEC Reliance 4MU3R/Alexander Y Type C49F that was purchased new by The Scottish Co-operative Wholesale Society, Glasgow, in June 1965. It was later transferred to the Aurs Road depot used by SCWS subsidiary Smith's of Barrhead. It was sold out of service in 1970 and Jimmy Edgar of Lochwinnoch took it in June 1971. It was snapped on a hire for Kennedy's Bar, Paisley, and is seen parked up at Saltcoats. By March 1975 it had moved to Galloway's of Harthill.

MNS 10Y was a Leyland Tiger TRBTL11/2R/Alexander TE Type C49F new as Central Scottish LT10 in April 1983. It passed to Kelvin Central Buses briefly as fleet number 2217, then moved to Fife Scottish as their 470 in 1989. Galloways of Harthill acquired it and adapted the former Stagecoach livery to produce a very tidy combination.

E396 MVV was an LAG Panoramic C49Ft that was purchased new by Grangeburn of Motherwell in March 1988 and was used on a daily express service linking Glasgow and Manchester Airport under the brand name of SCOT-MAN. Grangeburn Coaches were owned by the Nolan family, who later owned Bal-Na-Gask (Holdings) Ltd, which traded as Go Well Coaches.

PAG 903 was a Leyland Tiger Cub PSUC1/2/Duple Donnington C41F that was delivered new to Garnock Valley Motors of Kilbirnie in May 1960. It passed with the business to Paterson's of Dalry in 1975. Included in the deal were premises in Kilbirnie and eleven vehicles. GV held contracts for the MOD in Beith, which called for twelve vehicles every day.

MRR 473K was a Bedford YRQ/Duple Viceroy Express C45F that was purchased new by Makemson of Hucknall in May 1972. It passed to Aberfeldy Coaches as their fleet number 2 before reaching Silverdale Coaches of Airdrie. It then moved to John Campbell of East Kilbride in 1986. This picture shows it working as a duplicate for the fledgling Stagecoach of Perth company, and was taken in Glasgow.

Hutchison's of Overtown favoured the AEC Reliance for both its bus and coaching needs. UGB 15R was a 6U3ZR model fitted with a Plaxton Supreme C51Ft body. It was captured in Blackpool when it was brand new in April 1977. It would pass to Nationwide of Lanark in June 1980, then Travelong of South Ruslip in December 1984.

TNM 330K was an AEC Reliance 6MU4R/Duple Viceroy C53F that was purchased new by Charles Cook of Biggleswade in August 1971. It was purchased by Irvine's of Law before reaching Galloway's of Harthill in 1978, and was a stunning coach in its day. It was seen in the company of GMB 903K, which was new to the Godfrey Abbott Group.

YPD 139Y was a Leyland Tiger TRCTL11/2R/Duple Dominant IV Express C53F that was purchased new by London Country as their fleet number TD39 in June 1983 for use on National Express coach services. The batch was leased from Kirkby (dealers), and returned for refurbishment before resale. On disposal in June 1990 it passed to Smith's of Coupar, Angus, and was seen working into Perth on a service from Blairgowrie.

JNH 182Y was a Leyland Leopard PSU3G/4R/ECW B51 C46F new as United Counties number 182 in January 1983. The company was split up operationally from 1 January 1986 and this coach passed to Luton & District, which was privatised in August 1987. On disposal it passed to Milligan's of Mauchline, and was snapped in Kilmarnock.

LCX 160W was an AEC Reliance 6U3ZR/Plaxton Supreme IV Express C53F that was purchased new by Traject Ltd, t/a Abbeyways/Ivesways, of Huddersfield in March 1981, and was later fitted with a much rebuilt Paramount windscreen and side mouldings. It passed to Docherty's Midland Coaches of Auchterarder, who began in 1947 after investing in a single Bedford bus.

EUF 209D was a Leyland Leopard PSU3/3RT/Plaxton Panorama C49F new as Southdown number 1209 in July 1966. It was transferred to Bristol Omnibus before disposal to Marbill Coaches of Beith. Marbill Coaches was started in 1980 by Margaret and Bill Jackson, and had its roots in the earlier Jackson of Beith business.

UVD 313N was an AEC Reliance 6U3ZR/Van Hool Vistadome C49F new to Park's of Hamilton in October 1974, although it was a cancelled order for Eynon's of Trimsaran. It passed to Harris of Armadale and is seen leaving Glasgow on a tour. Van Hool was founded in 1947 by Bernard van Hool in Koningshooikt, near Lier, in Belgium.

WJS 840X was a Volvo B58-56/Plaxton Supreme VI C44Ft that was purchased new by Newton's of Dingwall in December 1981, although it was re-registered as 3692 NT for a spell. On disposal it became HAS 716X and passed to Skill's of Nottingham as their fleet number 19, before being sold to Gordon's of Rotherham in 1988. Newton's sold out to the Scottish Bus Group in December 1985.

Perhaps the flagship of all coaches ever operated by Grangeburn Coaches of Motherwell, G385 JBD was a LAG EOS E180Z C53Ft bought new in April 1990, and it was a stunner! Grangeburn was owned by the Nolan family from the 1950s until operations ceased in the early 1990s, although the company still exists as a holding company.

J. & H. Harkin's of Glasgow operated a chain of travel agents in the city, trading as Universal Travel, and this provided work for their coaches. FUS 243X was a Leyland Leopard PSU5C/4R/Plaxton Supreme IV C57F bought new in April 1982 and was photographed on a day tour to Dunoon, with the Firth of Clyde providing the backdrop. It would later pass to P. J. Travel of Dalmuir.

PSU 619 was a Kassbohrer Setra S215HR C53F purchased new by Silver Coach Lines of Edinburgh in April 1989. The name 'Setra' comes from '*selbsttragend*' (self-supporting). This refers to the integral nature of the construction of the vehicles manufactured from the 1950s to date. Originating on 16 June 1978 as Silver Fox Coaches, and then Silver Coach Lines Ltd, the company was then bought out by the Eirebus Group in Dublin to merge with their Edinburgh-based coach company Edinburgh Castle Coaches. In January 2005, it officially changed its name to Edinburgh Coach Lines Ltd.

ALR 455B was a Leyland Leopard L2/Harrington Cavalier C41F that was purchased new by the George Ewer Group, London, N16, in May 1964. The company traded as Grey-Green and was based on George Ewer's horse carriage business, which had been founded in 1885. The business prospered, and summer-only services were soon operating to the many South Coast resorts. This coach passed to Stokes of Carstairs, who sadly ceased operating in 2010.

A320 FHN was a Volvo B10M-61/LAG Galaxy C49Ft that was delivered new to Flear of Middlesbrough in October 1983. On disposal it passed to Beaton's of Blantyre. LAG were a Belgian coachbuilder whose main product was building tanker semi-trailers, but in the 1980s they diversified into coaches. Sadly, Beaton's ceased operations in 2004.

5642 UB was an AEC Reliance 2MU3RA/Plaxton Panorama C41C that was purchased new by Wallace Arnold Tours of Leeds in March 1960. It passed to Keenan of Coalhall and ran until the mid-1970s. The Plaxton Panorama, with forty-one seats as standard, was introduced at the 1958 Commercial Motor Show, as an addition to the existing range, available only on underfloor-engined chassis.

KM02 GSM was a Volvo B10M-62/Berkhof Axial C51Ft that was delivered new to Mayne's of Buckie in March 2002. It passed to Stokes of Carstairs in 2004 and was re-registered as WSU 864, and was captured on an Urquhart tour to Dunoon. On the demise of Stokes in 2010, it passed to Tramontana Coaches of Carfin.

OHE 268X was a Volvo B10M-61/Duple Goldliner C50F that was purchased new by National Travel (East) in June 1982, but was re-registered as UTC 872. On disposal it passed to Allander Travel of Milngavie as YFJ 67X, before moving to Marbill of Beith. Strangely, it returned to Allander for a second time, and was re-registered yet again, this time as CBZ 4622.

C345 GSD is a Volvo C10M-70 with Ramseier and Jenzer C48Ft coachwork which was built
in Switzerland for Park's of Hamilton in March 1986. It was photographed in Blantyre depot.
Only ten C10Ms were registered in the UK and six of them ended up with Park's. These vehicles
were very unusual in having a 7-metre wheelbase.

E404 LPR was a Duple 425 SDA1513 C53Ft that was delivered new to Ron's European of
Ashington in November 1987, and was later re-registered as MIL 1846. It passed to Huggins &
Simmons of Moreton, then moved to Williamson's of Knockin Heath in September 1998.
It returned to Huggins & Simmons before reaching Milligan's of Mauchline. On disposal it
became MAZ 6509 with AKM Coaches of Glasgow.

GSB 571 was a Bedford SB/Duple Super Vega C41F that was purchased new by Gold Line of Dunoon in 1961, and later passed to West Coast Motors. Since its inception in the 1920s West Coast has remained privately owned by the Craig family, and is headquartered in Campbeltown, Argyll. It now employs 400 staff and has a fleet of 220 buses and coaches. The company incorporates the following brands: City Sightseeing Glasgow, Bute & Oban, Glasgow Citybus, Kintyre Express, West Coast Tours, Fairline Coaches Ltd, and Borders Buses.

M555 GSM was a Dennis Javelin 12SDA/Berkhof C53F that was purchased new by Mayne's of Buckie in March 1995. Mayne's Coaches is a family owned business that has been trading since 1947, and was awarded Medium Coach Operator of the Year 2017 and Overall UK Coach Operator of the Year 2017 at the UK Coach Awards on 4 May. This coach later became PIL 8379 with Edward's Coaches of Llantwit Fardre.

TGD 995R was a Volvo B58-56/Plaxton Viewmaster C53F that was delivered new to Park's of Hamilton as their fleet number 15 in March 1977. Douglas Park founded the business in 1971 as a bus and coach operation with three vehicles. They now have in excess of 420 coaches and a supply of VIP coaches for most Central Scotland-based Scottish Premier League football teams. They also operate express coach services under contract to National Express, Megabus and Scottish Citylink, as well as operating their own city-to-city services.

B918 CSU was a Volvo B10M-61/Irizar Pyrenean C49Ft that was purchased new by Greyhound of Arbroath in May 1985, and was later re-registered as LXI 2630. It was supplied by Douglas Telfer's Tramontana organisation, which imported small numbers of Pyrenean coaches – a model derived from the coach sold in Spain as the Everest. Greyhound sold their coach fleet to the Tayside Public Transport Co. Ltd in 1990.

ONK 647H was a Leyland Leopard PSU3A/4R/Plaxton Elite C45F that was purchased new by World Wide Coaches of London, which was part of the Ewer Group, in June 1970. When George Ewer wanted a Scottish presence they bought out Whiteford's of Lanark and changed the name to World Wide (Scotland) Ltd. After a few years they decided to concentrate on their core operations and quit Scotland, selling the company back to its former directors, who changed the name to Nationwide.

E469 YWJ was a Neoplan Skyliner N122/3 CH57/20Ct that was purchased new by NAT Holidays of Leeds in April 1988. It was re-registered as NDZ 7937 by London Northern in January 1994 and numbered SKY1. It reached Gardiner, t/a Silver Choice, of East Kilbride in 1995, and then joined Pride of the Clyde Coaches in 1996. On disposal it passed to Total Transport of Leicester for further service.

SIL 1102 was an Irisbus Iveco Eurorider 397E.12.35/Beulas Cygnus C49Ft that was purchased new by Silver Fox Coaches of Renfrew in July 2006. The company can trace its roots back to the 1950s and was owned by Tommy Simpson. By the 1970s J. Craib had taken control, but this changed when Donald and Dorothy McLardy bought the company. It had its roots in Glasgow before moving to its current address in Renfrew, and is now run by the next generation of the family.

WSR 197K was a Ford R192/Duple Viceroy Express C45F that was purchased new by Alexander, t/a Greyhound Arbroath, in February 1972. The firm took over the licences of Hunter & Nelson of Arbroath in 1961, providing a network of local services around the town and a base to expand from.

ESW 717Y was a Magirus-Deutz M260/Ayats Diana new in 1983 to Little's which moved on pretty quickly to Nationwide of Lanark. It passed round a number of operators in the London area, including Richardson of Stevenage, but re-registered as JXI 9142. Ayats is the trading name of Carrocerías Ayats SA, a Spanish-based coachbuilder, and was established in 1905 by Mr Juan Ayats in Arbúcies, Catalonia.

E30 SBO was a Kassbohrer Setra Rational S215HR C49Ft that was purchased new by Bebb's of Llantwit Fardre in March 1988, and it was captured on a private hire to Glasgow. It would become MIL 9145, then later ran as WIB 7189 for JJ's Coaches. Milligan's were established in 1948 and have grown into a smart operator. It is still a family business, and is now on the third generation.

MSD 724W was a Volvo B58-61/Plaxton Viewmaster IV C49Ft that was delivered new to A1 Service member Docherty's of Irvine in 1981. The company maintained a separate coach fleet under the title of Cosy Ha', using a grey livery, based on that of Webster Bros of Wigan. Sadly, the company ceased operations in November 2008.

KGA 87Y was Bedford YNT/Castrosua Brisa 300 C53F that was purchased new by Nationwide of Lanark in August 1982, and was seen on a hire to Murrayfield Stadium in Edinburgh. On disposal it passed to Field's of Doncaster, t/a Terry's. Nationwide sold out to Wilson's of Carnwath, who continued the name for a few years before dropping it.

D477 DSX was a Van Hool Alicron T815 C55F that was delivered new to Wilson's of Carnwath in February 1987. The Wilson family started operating buses in the 1920s in the Galashiels area before moving to Carnwath. Many other Lanarkshire firms were taken over from the 1970s onwards, but the largest takeover was Nationwide of Lanark in 1990.

FLS 862V was a Leyland Leopard PSU3C/4R/Plaxton Supreme C53F that was purchased new by King's of Dunblane in March 1980. King's sold out to Rennie's of Dunfermline in the 1970s and were run as a subsidiary, maintaining their own identity. The use of lightweight coaches led to maintenance issues and the company was returned to the ownership of Charlie King. A new policy of using heavyweight Leyland chassis was undertaken, with a new coach being purchased most years.

HRC 102C was a Leyland Tiger Cub PSUC1/11T/Alexander Y Type C41F new as Trent 102 in December 1965. It passed to Morrison's of Castletown in 1981 and is seen at their depot. Sadly, the firm closed down in 2000. A total of 3,270 Y Type bodies were built between 1962 and 1983, including a small number built at Alexander's Belfast subsidiary.

KVD 443P was one of a batch of ten Leyland Leopard PSU3C/4R/Plaxton Elite C53Fs that was purchased new by Guards of London, W1, in September 1975, and supplied by Arlington Motors (dealer). It passed to Ayres of Dalkeith, and was on a hire to Glasgow when photographed. The firm was later rebranded as Postillion Coaches.

D411 FSX was a Bedford YNV Venturer/Duple 320 C57F that was delivered new to Prentice of West Calder in May 1987, and was seen in Glasgow. The Bedford Y series was first announced in September 1970, with the engine mounted centrally under the floor. The 12-metre YNV Venturer with air suspension was the final development of the Y series, and was announced in 1984. All bus and truck production by Bedford ceased in 1986.

B490 GBD was a Quest 80/Jonckheere C33Ft built as a demonstrator for Quest, Telford, in November 1983. Quest built a range of coach chassis featuring Ford Marine engines placed at the rear of their chassis. They made little impact on the market and quietly faded away after a couple of years. B490 GBD was registered by Roselare (dealers), who also went into receivership, leaving some partially completed coaches lying around. Stewart's of Dalkeith were Ford main dealers and thought that they could get some use from the breed, purchasing a few cheaply. B490 GBD was on a hire to Glasgow when snapped.

HSU 273N was a Ford R1014/Plaxton Elite III C45F that was delivered new to Barrie's of Balloch in March 1975. It carries the dark blue stripe which was added to the livery from 1973 onwards. On disposal in 1979 it moved to Gilchrist of East Kilbride. Barrie's built up a lot of MOD contracts, and the business never recovered after they were lost to other operators.

EBR 850S was a Seddon Pennine VII/Plaxton Supreme C53F that was purchased new by OK Motor Services of Bishop Auckland in May 1978, and was the only one taken by an independent to bus-grant specification. It later passed to Mitchell's of Plean before reaching Allison's of Dunfermline. It was built alongside a batch of similar coaches for Eastern Scottish.

EYS 995C was an AEC Reliance 2MU4RA/Duple (Northern) C41F that was purchased new by Cotter's Tours of Glasgow in June 1965. It passed to Gibson's of Moffat in October 1969 and served until 1974, when it was traded into Yeates (dealers). It appeared with Grice & Kidd of Crawley in June 1975, and moved to Nesbit Bros of Somerby the following year.

J466 NJU was a Dennis Javelin/Caetano C53F that was purchased new by Aron of Northolt in April 1992. It joined the Owen's of Chapelhall fleet as NIL 4989 for use on their Scottish Highway Express operations, which very successfully grabbed a share of the Glasgow to Edinburgh express market. The operations were sold to Stagecoach, who kept the name for a little while before running under their own identity.

MSG 914T was a Volvo B58-58/Plaxton Supreme C49F that was purchased new by Allan's of Gorebridge in May 1979, and is shown on a hire to Bellahouston Park in Glasgow. Allan's have been in business for over eighty years, and are still going strong. This coach passed to Wilson's of Carnwath in 1986 for further service.

F452 FKY was a Volvo B10M-61/Ikarus Blue Danube C53F that was purchased new by Allander Travel of Milngavie in May 1989. It was re-registered as 2154 K, then changed to F442 YSJ. The body was letting in water so the decision was made to rebody it in January 1993 with Van Hool Alizee C48Ft coachwork. It was re-registered yet again to CXI 987. It passed to Brown's of Edinburgh, then Prentice Westwood, where it became 81 CBK. By 2010 it was with Destinations of Harthill as JHZ 4802.

B836 FTY was a Bedford YNT/Duple Laser C53F that was purchased new by Cox, t/a Gypsy Queen, of Langley Park in December 1984. It passed to Dunnet's of Keiss and was snapped in Thurso while working on the service to Wick. They also provided coaches for the 'Fast Class' consortium on the Inverness/Wick/Thurso corridor. The Rapson Group took the firm over in 1992.

USB 159M was a Ford R1014/Willowbrook Expressway 002 C45F that was that was delivered new to Bowman's of Craignure in August 1973, and is shown awaiting the arrival of the ferry from Oban. On disposal it passed to Palmer of Carlisle, then Allways of Chatham. Bowman's operated on the Isle of Mull and were taken over by West Coast Motors on 24 June 2013.

JCS 200N was an AEC Reliance 6MU4R/Willowbrook Expressway 002 DP49F that was purchased new by AA Motor Services member Dodd's of Troon as their DT12 in June 1975. It was a bus-grant-assisted purchase and had to spend 50 per cent of its first seven years on stage-carriage services. This often meant a turn on the Prestwick Airport to Glasgow service. It was sold in January 1983 to Mathews Blue Coaches of Shouldham and then Mike DeCourcey Travel of Coventry in July 1984.

WUS 691S was a Volvo B58-56/Plaxton Supreme C51F, new in August 1977 to Golden Eagle of Salsburgh. On disposal it went to Marshall's of Baillieston and then McKenna of Uddingston before reaching King of Kirkcowan. It was captured on a football hire to Paisley. Golden Eagle Coaches started in business in 1926. Peter Irvine, the founder and grandfather of the present owners, was a former miner.

XSV 270 was a Volvo B10M-62/Van Hool Alizee C38F that was delivered new to Mackie's of Alloa in April 1995. It passed to Marbill of Beith and was re-registered as 2154 K in June 2006. It became M821 YSC and ran for Kings/ABC Travel of Castle Douglas. It was snapped on the A9 near Moy in the Highlands. The business, which runs a fleet of over twenty vehicles, was established in 1949 by David Mackie, the father of the present owner.

HYS 53N was a Volvo B58-61/Plaxton Elite C57F that was purchased new by Park's of Hamilton in March 1975, shown in Blackpool. It would later pass to Buddens Coaches in Wiltshire. The coach division was strengthened in 1996 with the acquisition of Trathens Travel Services Ltd, an express coach operator incorporating Star Riders and based in Plymouth.

WJS 199X was a Volvo B58-56/Plaxton Supreme C45F that was purchased new by Morris Newton of Dingwall in August 1981. It passed to Hutchison's of Overtown in July 1984, and was upseated to C53F. It joined Browning's in April 1985 and, it must be said, looked supreme. It moved to Mason's of Bo'ness in August 1986, then Mitchell's of Plean in April 2001, and finally Russell's of Glasgow in 2002.

CAG 442C was a Leyland Leopard PSU3/3R/Alexander Y Type C49F that was purchased new by Western SMT as their fleet number L2027 in June 1966. It was transferred to Central SMT as their T406 in 1981 and was fitted with bus seats. It was sold to Marbill and was being used during the visit of Pope John Paul II to Glasgow in 1982.

YSN 335T was a Bedford YMT/Plaxton Supreme IV Express C53F that was purchased new by TD Alexander, t/a Greyhound, of Arbroath in March 1979. The owner of the company was T. D. Alexander, a nephew of Walter Alexander of bus fame. The firm also had bases in Dundee and Sheffield, and buses were often swapped around.

PVO 21X was a Volvo B58-61/Duple Dominant III C57F new as Skill's of Nottingham fleet number 21 in August 1981. On disposal it passed to McKechnie's of Bathgate. The Duple Dominant III had shallow, parallelogram-shaped side windows and was designed for the Glasgow to London service of the Scottish Bus Group, although it was also made available to other operators.

D898 TGG was a Bedford YNV/Wright Contour C57F that was delivered new to Prentice of West Calder in May 1987. Wrights of Ballymena produced a coach body for the UK market, which was ahead of its time in using Alusuisse aluminium construction and given the name Contour. There were only thirty-seven Wright Contour bodies produced.

SWW 134R was a Leyland Leopard PSU3E/4R with Duple Dominant II C53F coachwork, new in April 1977 to Wallace Arnold of Leeds. On disposal it passed to Cosgrove, t/a Tay Valley Coaches, of Dundee who used it on WA feeder services from Scotland. The Dominant II was introduced in 1976 and had a deeper windscreen, rectangular headlights and a flat rear window.

UAR 932M was an AEC Reliance 6U3ZR/Plaxton Elite C53F that was purchased new by Limebourne Coaches of London, SW1, in March 1974. It passed to Capital Coaches of London before reaching Miller's of Calderbank. Miller's livery was inspired by second-hand vehicles purchased from Shearings Holidays, and the firm continues to operate. It passed to Letham's of Blantyre in 1985 for further service.

B925 BGA was a Volvo B10M-53/Plaxton Paramount 4000 CH55/9Ft that was purchased new by Newton's of Dingwall in April 1985. It passed with the business to the Scottish Bus Group in December 1985 and briefly ran for Highland before transfer to Western, where it would be re-registered to WLT 447 in May 1990. It became B931 EGG in November 1992 when it was sold to Marbill of Beith, and by 1993 it had become PJI 2845. It then ran for HAD Coaches of Shotts. It has also run for Brighton Blue Bus, Thandi Coaches, Crawley Luxury Coaches and Garnett's of Bishop Auckland, and became B10 TMT later in its life.

HSD 708N was a Volvo B58-61/Alexander M Type C42Ft that was purchased new by Western SMT as their V2537 in May 1975 for use on the London to Scotland service. It was rebuilt with jack-knife doors before resale to Lyles of Batley, then Fourseasons Coaches of Leeds. It passed to John Chapman, t/a Silverdale, of Airdrie.

SFS 496Y was a Bova Europa EL26/581 C53F that was purchased new by Mason's of Bo'ness in February 1983, shown working on hire to Western SMT. It passed to Silver Fox Coaches of Renfrew before joining Tilley's of Wainhouse as GIL 3579. J. D. Bots, later to be known as J. D. Bova, started the company that would come to be known as Bova in 1878 with the creation of a timber business in Valkenswaard. When J. D. Bots died, he left the business to his eldest son, Simon, who first introduced the name Bova, which was derived from Bots Valkenswaard.

B670 GBD was a DAF MB200/Caetano Algarve C53F that was delivered new to Trathen of Roborough in March 1985. It passed to Midland Fox as their fleet number 8009 before reaching Whyte's of Newmacher in 1989 and was photographed on a visit to Glasgow. It would later join Town & Country Coaches. Whytes continue to operate their own program of coach holidays.

A145 JTA was a Volvo B10M-61/Berkhof Esprite C49Ft new to Trathen's of Yelverton as their fleet number 45 in March 1985. It passed to Baker's of Yeovil before reaching Marshall's of Baillieston. It was purchased by A1 Coaches of Methilhill before moving to Prentice Westwood in 1996. The Prentice fleet has a pedigree stretching back around seventy years.

G845 GNV was a Volvo B10M-60/Jonckheere Deauville C51Ft that was purchased new by Green's of Kirkintilloch in September 1989 to launch their Glasgow to Edinburgh service. This ran in partnership with Silver Coach Lines of Edinburgh but was not successful. This coach passed to Marbill of Beith, then Shropshire Bus & Coach, where it became 607 EXA.

PXI 5517/23 are Leyland Tiger TRCTL11/3ARZA/Alexander (Belfast) TE Type C53Fs that were purchased new by Ulsterbus as their fleet numbers 517/523 in April 1990. On disposal they passed to Dodd's of Troon before moving to Shuttle Buses of Kilwinning. Shuttle Buses is owned by Dave Granger and nowadays separate their coaching activities under the Shuttle Coaches brand.

E218 GNV was a Volvo B10M-61/Jonckheere Deauville C51Ft new to The Londoners in September 1987. It was acquired by Silver Fox of Glasgow and used on Scottish Citylink duties. It passed to John Morrow of Clydebank in 1993, where it became 216 TYC, and has also served with Hills of Stibb Cross and Alpha of Honiton. It has carried quite a few other registrations, including E754 NWP, B6 GBD and FIG 6431.

FJ04 ESU was a Volvo B12M/Sunsundeguidi C49Ft that was purchased new by Rennie's of Dunfermline in May 2004, and was caught in Castle Esplanade in Edinburgh. In March 2008, it was announced that Stagecoach Fife had bought Rennie's of Dunfermline for an undisclosed sum. The Rennie fleet comprised sixty vehicles, and included eighteen double-deckers, which were all leased from Stagecoach in Fife.

WTG 64T was a Leyland Leopard PSU3E/4R/Duple Dominant II C51F new as Newport Corporation fleet number 64 in August 1978. It passed to Henderson's of Carstairs, and then Alan Dickson of Dumfries purchased it in 1987 and re-registered it as SW 8480. It then passed to Whitelaw's of Stonehouse for spares, which allowed the registration number to be transferred to Sandra Whitelaw's Mercedes car.

D804 SGB was a Volvo B10M-61/Plaxton Paramount C49Ft that was purchased new by Park's of Hamilton in May 1987. It passed to Clyde Coast Services in June 1988, and was re-registered as 4504 RU the following year. Charlie Riddler of Arbroath acquired it in January 1992, and it was caught in St Andrew Square in Edinburgh.

A145 JTA was a Volvo B10M-61/Berkhof Esprite C49Ft new to Trathen's of Yelverton as their fleet number 45 in March 1985. It passed to Baker's of Yeovil before reaching Marshall's of Baillieston who, it must be said, did a superb job on it. It looks like a brand-new vehicle as it passes Glasgow's Tollcross Park. Marshall's always ran an immaculate fleet.

WAO 17H was a Ford R226/Plaxton Elite C53F that was purchased new by Gordon's of Kirkbride in July 1970. On disposal in 1972 it passed to Hunter's of Loanhead before reaching Rae's of Waterloo in 1975. The company ceased around 1980, with son Andy leaving to work for Hutchison's of Overtown.

XCU 421M was an AEC Reliance 6U3ZR/Plaxton Elite C57F that was delivered new to Mallam of South Shields in August 1973. It was acquired by Harris of Armadale and was working on hire to Scottish Citylink when seen. It later joined Redwatch Coaches of East Calder. The Harris brothers disappeared without a trace over the festive season of 1988, abandoning the business.

TND 407X was a DAF MB200DKTL/Plaxton Supreme V C51F new as Jackson's of Altrincham fleet number 407 in April 1982. On disposal it joined Supreme of Hadleigh before reaching EVE Coaches of Dunbar in 1988. It would pass to Steele's of Stevenston in 1990. Jackson's were part of the Shearings Group, and were a rich source of second-hand coaches over the years.

C44 KHS was a MAN 16.280/Berkhof C53F built as a demonstrator for Tony Andrews (dealer) in April 1986. The company was associated with Hutchison's Overtown, so it came as no surprise when it joined their fleet. On disposal in 1989 it passed to Bob Chapman of Airdrie, t/a Gold Circle. It later worked for Armstrong's of Linlithgow and Mayne's of Buckie, where it became YSU 990.

JRY 569V was a Volvo B58-56/Plaxton Supreme C53F that was delivered new to International Coaches of Thornton Heath in March 1980. The chassis was bought from Blythswood (dealers) in Glasgow and sent to Plaxton's to be fitted with a new Paramount 3200 body. It is shown at Milngavie after its return with its new registration number, 3786 AT.

FHS 726X was a Volvo B10M-61/Duple Goldliner C51Ft that was purchased new by Park's of Hamilton in April 1982. It would later be re-registered to HIL 6580 and serve with Delta Coaches of Stockton and Orr of Paisley. The Duple Goldliner was introduced in 1981 to compete with the earlier Plaxton Viewmaster. It retained the front of a Dominant but had varying raised body styles – II, III and IV.

C769 MVH was a DAF MB200DKFL/Plaxton Paramount 3500 C53F that was purchased new by Smith's of Alcester in March 1986. It passed to Mayne's of Buckie and was re-registered as YXI 3410, as shown in this view taken in Union Street in Aberdeen. The firm have been in business since 1947, when James Mayne began running coaches after two years of operating a local taxi, car and limousine hire business.

L906 NWW was a Volvo B10M-60/Van Hool Alizee C48Ft that was delivered new to Wallace Arnold Tours of Leeds in March 1994. On disposal it joined Leon's of Stafford before reaching Spa Coaches of Strathpeffer in 1997. It was re-registered as PAZ 2535, and was photographed taking a break near Pitlochry. The firm operate their own coach tours programme.

PNR 101G was a Bedford VAM70/Caetano Cascais C45F new as Hargreaves of Morley number 101 in March 1969. It passed to William McClure of Glenmavis and was seen on a visit to Ayr. It was acquired by Wilson's of Carnwath in 1973 along with a works contract, and later saw service with Pavena of Livingston.

KSK 978 was a Volvo B10M-62/Jonckheere Deauville C53F that was delivered new to Park's of Hamilton in February 1995. It was re-registered as M994 HHS on disposal to Smith's of Keith, and was caught in Carrbridge. It then moved to JP Coaches of Forfar before passing to Fishers Tours of Dundee, where it was re-registered as RJI 2718 and upseated to C70F for a school contract.

LCB 924P was owned by Robert Sweetin of Crosshouse. It had begun in life as North Western Road Car Company fleet number 962, registered as VDB 962. It was a Leyland Leopard PSU3/3R/Plaxton C51F that was new in December 1962. It was rebodied by Plaxton in April 1976 with this Elite C53F body, which was built to the requirements of Fairclough of Radcliffe, t/a Tatlocks, and, just to really confuse people, it was also fitted with a Leyland Panther badge.

C215 BOS was a Scania K112TR/Plaxton Paramount 4000 CH55/16Ct new as Western Scottish LA215 in June 1986. It was later re-registered as VLT 81, then C918 MGB. It passed to McDade's of Uddingston in 1991 as RJI 1650. It later passed to Lewis Coaches of Rotherham for further service. The Paramount 4000 double-decker coach was initially built on Neoplan underframes, but it was later also offered on Scania and DAF chassis.

GJH 714L was a Ford R226/Caetano Estoril C53F new to Welwyn Garden City Coaches of St Albans in August 1972. It passed to Robb's of Brechin and was caught on a visit to Glasgow. Salvador Caetano bodywork was imported to the UK by Alf Moseley, and sold well because the lightweight chassis paired with the Continental bodywork was one of the cheapest combinations on the market at the time.

PAR 823H was a Bedford VAS5/Duple Vista 25 C29F new to the National Cash Register Company, London, NW1, in May 1970, but was possibly used at their Dundee plant. It was acquired by Thomson's of Dundee and is shown on a football hire to Glasgow. Thomson's ran a lightweight fleet of around eight coaches at any given time.

XWX 199S was a Volvo B58-56/Plaxton Supreme C53F that was delivered new to Wallace Arnold Tours of Leeds in April 1978. It was part of a batch of four that featured Pneumocyclic gearboxes and Telma retarders and were bought for evaluation. This one passed to Smith, t/a Croft Coaches, of Dalmellington.

ERM 807K was a Ford R192/Duple Viceroy Express C45F new as Cumberland fleet number 807 in August 1972. This was an unusual choice for a member of the National Bus Company, but was built to bus-grant specification. On disposal it passed to Pencaitland Garage, and was captured in Glasgow.

SWW 137R was a Leyland Leopard PSU3E/4R/Duple Dominant II C53F that was purchased new by Wallace Arnold Tours of Leeds in April 1977. It passed to David Syme of Bearsden, who was an owner-driver and a familiar sight in the Glasgow area for many years. Normally, only a couple of vehicles were owned at any time.

DKS 20X was a Volvo B10M-56/Plaxton Supreme V GT Express C53F that was purchased new by R. J. Nichol in April 1982 and is seen in its home town of Hawick. It was an immaculate fleet and vehicles were much sought after second-hand. This one was snapped up by Marshall's of Baillieston in 1988 and re-registered as 7617 SM before sale to McNairn's of Coatbridge in 1999, although it returned to its original registration plate.

POD 416M was a Volvo B58-56/Plaxton Elite C51F that was delivered new to Trathen's of Yelverton in April 1974. It passed to Beaton's of Blantyre and received this 'mock' Park's livery to match some recently acquired coaches. It would pass to Eagle Coaches of Stevenston for further service.

JLS 4V was a MAN SR280 C53F that was purchased new by Park's of Hamilton in May 1980 and is shown in their Hamilton depot. The MAN SR280 gave 280 bhp, and was produced between 1975 and 1984, with Park's taking a batch of ten. They were delivered in the new cream-based livery.

B567 LSC was a Leyland Tiger TRCTL11/3RH/Duple Caribbean 2 C46Ft new as Eastern Scottish XCL 567 in April 1985. It passed to Rowe's of Muirkirk, and was arriving in Cumnock when seen. It also worked for MacTavish Coaches of Dalmuir. Rowe's later merged with Tudhope Coaches of Kilmarnock.

F973 HGE was a Volvo B10M-60/Plaxton Paramount C53F that was purchased new by Park's of Hamilton in February 1989, and is seen in Drumnadrochit. It became JSK 261 with Plymouth Citycoach. The coach was operating when photographed for Trafalgar Tours, which is owned by the Travel Corporation. The corporation has been in business since 1947 and has offices in Australia, Canada, China, New Zealand, Singapore, South Africa, the UK and the USA, operating guided tours across six continents.

RSN 317H was a Ford R192/Plaxton Elite C45F that was delivered new to Barrie's of Balloch in November 1967, and featured the lion rampart transfers applied from 1967 onwards. The fleet from the mid-1960s onwards featured lightweight chassis and would be changed over two years or so. Sadly, the company closed down on 25 April 1988 after the owner suffered ill health.

TGD 981R was a Volvo B58-61/Plaxton Supreme C57F new to Park's of Hamilton in March 1977 and is seen after joining Marshall's of Baillieston's immaculate fleet. Marshall's ran an immaculate fleet, with blue being the preferred livery, but sometimes other operators' colours were retained, with the signwriting suitably altered.

B252 CVX was a DAF MB200DKFL/Duple Laser 2 C57F new as Southend Transport fleet number 252 in June 1985. It was acquired by Keenan of Coalhall in 1993 and was re-registered as AEF 91A. The Laser was introduced in 1982 and resembled the Dominant, but with a rounder front and body-coloured front grille. The new design did little to halt the slide in production, and in 1983 Duple output was just 340 bodies.

JFM 475N was a Leyland Leopard PSU3B/4R/Duple Dominant C53F that was purchased new by Bostock's of Congleton in April 1975. It passed to Law's of Bucksburn, then Beaton's of Blantyre before reaching Allander Travel of Milngavie in 1986, where it received a Plaxton Paramount front end.

SMS 833H was a Bedford VAS5/Duple Vista 25 C29F new as Alexander (Midland) MW 293 in June 1970. It was transferred to Highland Omnibuses as their CD94 in 1977 before passing to Penman Bros of Glasgow. From 1968 Duple coach production was concentrated at Blackpool, and the Hendon factory finally closed in 1970.

George Paterson of Hamilton acquired SSK 694X from Barrie's of Balloch in 1986, although it had been purchased new by Dunnet's of Keiss. It was a Bedford YNT/Duple Dominant IV C53F, and was captured at Duple Coachbuilders' Barrhead Repair Centre. It was fitted with a Cummins engine and would remain in the fleet until 1994.

OAG 214L was a UTIC U2043 C53F that was purchased new by John Woods of Largs in 1972. Portuguese manufacturer UTIC was well-known for building vehicles based on AEC running units over a considerable period of years. A small batch of nine UTIC U2043 integrals were imported into the UK by Loughborough dealer Moseley's. OAG 214L passed to Premier of Titchmarsh in 1976, then went to Richard's of Brynmawr for further service.

Fife-based operator Norman Hall ran a Saturday service from Glasgow to Anstruther Holiday Village. Unusually, he purchased two ex-SBG Alexander M Type Coaches. MSF 751P was a Seddon Pennine VII that was purchased new by Eastern Scottish as their XS 751 in June 1976, while HOI 2319 was a Volvo B58-61 that was purchased new by Western SMT as HSD 706N in May 1975.

J2 DTS was a Neoplan Skyliner N122/3 CH77Ct that was purchased new by Durham Travel Services in November 1991. It passed to Moffat & Williamson in 1998 and was re-registered to YBK 159. On disposal it joined Prentice Westwood as YRR 436 and later IUI 2129. Alongside is similar BSK 789, which was new as K302 JTS to Express Travel of Perth in 1993. It would become Maghull Coaches 951 RMX in due course.

PGW 659L was a Leyland Leopard PSU3B/4R/Plaxton Elite C49F that was purchased new by Grey-Green, London, N16, in April 1973. On disposal it passed to Gilmours of Crosshouse before passing to Jack Waddell of Lochwinnoch. It subsequently passed to Eagle Coaches of Dunoon and was later destroyed in an arson attack.

RJS 191L was a Ford R1014/Willowbrook B52F that was purchased new by Newton's of Dingwall in 1973. On disposal it passed to Doig's Tours (Greenock) Ltd, before reaching Tennant's of Forth in 1977, and was used mainly on colliery contracts for the National Coal Board. Sadly, as this business declined over the years the company put most of their investment into haulage, and the bus side was phased out.

TNP 7V was a Volvo B58-61/Unicar C57F that was purchased new by Aston's of Kempsey in February 1980. It then passed to Caelloi Coaches in Wales before joining Irvine's of Law. It was photographed in Park's City Coach Terminal in Glasgow. It would later serve with Caldwell's of Greenock, Pride of the Clyde, and Beaton's of Blantyre. It was unusual for a Unicar body in having a Bristol Dome fitted.

NFS 172Y was a Leyland Leopard PSU3G/4R/Alexander T Type C49F new as Alexander (Fife) FPE172 in October 1982. It passed to Stagecoach with the business before being sold to Docherty's of Irvine. It then moved to Galloways of Harthill, then joined Marshall's of Baillieston in 2001, as shown here. It passed to Jay Coaches in 2003.

FBF 794H was a Bedford VAM70 with Duple Viceroy coachwork new as Harper Bros, Heath Hayes, fleet number 62 in May 1970. It passed to Midland Red with the business in 1974 as their 2262. It is shown after disposal to William O'Neill of Greenock on a football hire to Glasgow. In 1966 the Duple Viceroy range replaced the Bella series on most Bedford or Ford chassis.

K888 GSM was a Toyota Coaster HDB30R/Caetano Optimo C21F that was delivered new to Mayne's of Buckie in November 1992. The Toyota Coaster was introduced in 1969 as a seventeen-passenger minibus, using the same running gear as the Toyota Dyna of the time, and that was used on the Salvador Caetano Optimo sold in Western Europe. K888 GSM moved on to Colins Minicoaches for further service.

M268 POS was a Volvo B10M-62/Van Hool C53F that was purchased new by Henry Crawford of Neilston in September 1994. It passed to Long's Coaches of Salsburgh in 1999, and is shown in 'Motorvator' livery for use on a Glasgow to Edinburgh express service, which was worked jointly with Bruce of Salsburgh, using a common livery. The service was sold to Stagecoach in July 2004.

CJF 2T was a Volvo B58-61/Plaxton Supreme IV C50F that was purchased new by Kinch of Mountsorrel in April 1979. On disposal it passed to Dunn Coaches of Croydon. Barraclough, t/a Eagle Coaches, of Stevenston purchased it from Keenan of Coalhall in 1985, and it was captured on a private hire to Oban.

PUS 830M was an AEC Reliance 6U3ZR/Plaxton Elite C55F that was purchased new by Weir's Tours (Bowling) Ltd in April 1974. Weir's traditional livery was dark brown and gold, but this coach was delivered in this two-tone blue livery, which had been copied from two former Best of London vehicles already in the fleet. It would later pass to Wilson's of Carnwath for further service.

28 FAX was a Bristol MW6G/ECW C39F new as Red & White number UC6 in December 1962. On disposal in 1977 it passed to Gilmour's Coaches of Crosshouse, moving to Henry Crawford of Neilston the following year, only to return to Gilmour's. It is shown having a window replaced. Vehicles seemed to pass between these companies on a regular basis.

A very well-travelled Leyland Tiger with Plaxton Viewmaster body – new as THN 882X to Trimdon Motors – is seen here as JUI 4680 with Tommy Withers, t/a Ayrways, of Patna. It seems to have had at least another eight operators in between and five registrations! Tommy had begun running coaches as Ayrliners before adopting the Ayrways name.

B530 LSG was a Leyland Tiger TRCTL11/3RH/Alexander TC Type C53F that was purchased new by Silver Coach Lines of Edinburgh in April 1985 – a very unusual choice, explained by the fact that Alexander's owned the coach company. It passed to Docherty's of Auchterarder and became GSU 377. It later passed to Mitchell's of Plean and then Davies of Plean.

F231 DWF was a Volvo B10M-61/Plaxton Paramount 3200 C53F new as fleet number F1 of Fleet Coaches of Fleet in August 1988. On disposal in 1994 it passed to McGilvary of Acharacle, t/a Shiel Buses. The firm continues to thrive and nowadays has a second depot in Fort William, and operates around thirty-five vehicles. Coaches are provided for Scottish Citylink in the area.

OGE 208P was a Bedford YRQ/Duple Dominant C45F that was purchased new by Cadger of Balmedie in April 1976. It had moved to J. E. McMillan, t/a Sunningdale Coaches, of Giffnock by the time of this picture, however, and was captured in Edinburgh's Royal Mile. The fleet usually contained half a dozen coaches at any given time.

TFG 223X was one of a batch of three Leyland Leopard PSU5E/4Rs fitted with Plaxton Supreme V coachwork, which were new to Southdown Motor Services in June 1982. Later a member of the Brighton & Hove fleet, and utilised on National Holidays work, it was found at the depot of Stuart Shevill, t/a Stuarts, of Carluke in 1998.

VUD 29X was a Leyland Leopard PSU3G/4R/ECW C49F new as City of Oxford fleet number 29 in April 1992. It worked for South Midland before being sold to Fitzcharles of Grangemouth. It later passed to MacEwan's of Dumfries. Fitzcharles began selling bikes in 1929 and launched its popular coach hire, package holiday and tour business from there in 1946. Sadly, the business collapsed in October 2015.

C332 PEW was a Leyland Tiger TRCTL11/3RZ/Plaxton Paramount C53F new as Premier Travel fleet number 332 in March 1986. It was re-registered as HSV 194, and was then changed to C471 PEW for disposal. It passed to Andy Crawford, t/a Ann's Coaches, of Kirkintilloch and subsequently became 8402 AC. It was captured as it passed through Dumfries.

NYS 57Y was a Leyland Tiger TRCTL11/3R/Van Hool Alizee C52F new to Doig's Tours (Greenock) Ltd in May 1983 and is seen on a CIE tour of Scotland at Spean Bridge. The original owners sold the business to McDowall's of Glasgow. On the death of Mr McDowall in the early 1960s, the Doig's subsidiary was offered for sale as a going concern. It was bought by a haulage company by the name of S. & J. Harris, who incidentally owned one coach themselves.

SSB 816L was a Ford R192/Duple Viceroy Express C45F that was purchased new by Cowal Motors of Dunoon in April 1973. Cowal were associated with Baird's of Dunoon and were owned by the Graham family, who had previously operated in the Kirkintilloch area and had sold their bus services to Alexander's. It was sold to Preddy of Gloucester in 1986.

R918 ULA was a Volvo B10M-62/Bekhof Axial C49Ft that was purchased new by Q-Drive, Battersea, in February 1998. It passed to Earnside of Glenfarg the following year. The livery employed was inspired by York Pullman's colours, but has altered over the years, and currently uses a white base with yellow and maroon flashes.

4143 AT was a Van Hool Acron T818 CH6oFt that was purchased new in June 1983. It heads a high-quality line-up in Strothers Lane in Inverness. Allander and Newton's of Dingwall were partners in 'Fast Class' express coach operations, which linked Glasgow/Edinburgh/Perth to Inverness, with extensions to Thurso provided by Dunnet's of Keiss. Eventually the Scottish Bus Group bought Newton's business and entered into an agreement with Allander that if they took the service off, they were given a guaranteed mileage on Citylink work for a couple of years.

DJX 76D was an AEC Reliance 2MU3RA/Alexander Y Type C47F new as Hebble fleet number 76 in May 1966, and later came under the auspices of National Travel (North East). It was unusual in having the destination screen under the windscreen instead of on the front dome. It passed to Garelochhead Coach Services as their 132 in 1975, and is seen in a rather battered condition at the depot.

MSF 645X was a Volvo B10M-61/Duple Goldliner C53F that was purchased new by Stanley Mackay of Edinburgh in May 1982. I always admired this fleet, which was always well turned out, and I loved the metal sword attached to the side panels. It would finish its days with Simpson of Cockermouth. The Mackay business was absorbed by City Circle coaches to provide a Scottish base.

D501 BFS was an ACE Puma IV/Plaxton Paramount C39F that was built in September 1986 for Traject of Huddersfield, although it was never used or registered by them. It was taken by Ramsay's of Elsrickle, and was caught in Glasgow. It later became WAZ 3429 with Fargo Coachlines. Despite some vigorous marketing attempts by Traject Managing Director Steven Ives, little interest in the Puma coach was shown, with only twelve being built, and ACE Ltd closed down in 1992.

G450 DSB was a Volvo B10M-60/Duple 340 C55F that was purchased new by West Coast Motors for Scottish Citylink work in April 1990, and is shown arriving in Glasgow on the 926 service from Campbeltown. It later passed to Tanat Valley Coaches and was sadly lost in a depot fire at Llanrhaeadr-ym-Mochnant in autumn 2006. In July 1989, the decision was made to close down Duple Coachbuilders.

FSU 59T was a Ford R1014/Duple Dominant II C45F that was delivered new to Mitchell of Broxburn in January 1979. The Ford R series chassis evolved from designs made by Thames Trader until the mid-1960s. A number of components were shared with the D series lorry, including the engine, which was mounted vertically at the front of the vehicle, ahead of the front axle so as to provide a passenger entrance opposite the driver. The original R192 later became the R1014 variant (nominally 10 metres long with a 140 bhp engine).

AAG 702B was a Leyland Leopard PSU3/3RT/Plaxton Panorama C51F that was purchased new by Clyde Coast member Hugh Frazer in June 1964. It lasted until May 1976, when it passed to Jackson's of Beith and ran for around three years. It ended its days with a farmer in the Laurencekirk area.

PGD 996P was an AEC Reliance 6U3ZR/Plaxton Supreme C51F that was purchased new by Irvine's of Salsburgh, t/a Golden Eagle Coaches, in June 1976. It was caught in Blackpool on a private hire. It was withdrawn in 1984 and passed to Cheddar Valley Coaches of Sandford for further service. Golden Eagle recently celebrated their 90th anniversary in the business and are still going strong.

HSD 706N was a Volvo B58-61/Alexander M Type C42Ft that was purchased new by Western SMT as their fleet number V2535 in May 1975. On disposal it passed to Hall's of Kennoway, where this replacement front panel was fitted from a Plaxton Supreme. The low second-hand prices obtained for these buses led to SBG rebuilding many later Duple coaches before disposal. It is shown with Robb's of Brechin later in its life.

HYD 520K was a Seddon Pennine 6/Plaxton Elite C57F that was purchased new by Clevedon Motorways in March 1972. On disposal it passed to J. A. Gannon, t/a Abbot Travel, of Loanhead, near Edinburgh. The Pennine 6 chassis used a turbocharged Perkins six-cylinder engine, and was built in Oldham. In 1974 the firm was acquired by the American giant International Harvester, and in February 1983 it was purchased by the Spanish group ENASA, which made it a subsidiary of Pegaso. In 1990 it became part of the international commercial vehicle concern Iveco.

OEH 44M was a Ford R1114/Duple Dominant C51F new as Potteries Motor Traction fleet number 44 in June 1974. On disposal it passed to Meffan's of Kirrriemuir, but is shown with Petrie's of Blairgowrie on a hire to Glasgow. On disposal in 1986, it passed to MacEwan's of Dumfries.

PWB 658X was a Leyland Leopard PSU5C/4R/Duple Dominant IV C53F that was purchased new by Rennie's of Dunfermline in April 1982, and is seen on Blackpool Promenade during the 1982 coach rally. It would later become MSP 333, then MFS 579X. It was later acquired by Collins Coaches, Cambridge, before passing to Williams & Robinson, Scunthorpe.

LAK 307W was a DAF MB200DKTL/Plaxton Supreme C53F that was delivered new to Globe of Barnsley in June 1981. On disposal it passed to Austin's of Earlston before joining Robert Stewart, t/a Premier Coaches, of Renfrew. It was photographed arriving in Paisley on an express service from the National Savings Bank, which was based at Cowglen in Glasgow.

G850 VAY was a Dennis Javelin 8.5SDA/Plaxton Paramount C32Ft that was purchased new by Green's of Kirkintilloch in August 1989. It passed to Stokes of Carstairs in 1990 and was re-registered as WSU 860 in July 1991. William Stokes had begun operating in the 1920s and provided miners' transport to local pits along with two stage services based on Lanark. Sadly, Stokes went out of business in 2010.

DSJ 257V was a Bedford YMT/Unicar C53F that was delivered new to Kerr's of Galston in September 1979. It carried the name *Louden Princess* and was caught on a visit to Glasgow. Spanish Unicar coach bodies were available on Bedford YMT coach chassis from January 1979. Union Carrocera appointed Moseley Group (PSV) Ltd as its sole UK concessionaire for the model, which made its British debut at the Brighton Coach Rally.

D764 XFR was a Volvo B10M-61/Plaxton Paramount C49Ft that was delivered new to Cosgrove of Preston in February 1987. It passed to Rapson's Coaches of Alness in 1990, and was later re-registered as ESK 981. Rapson's purchased Highland Scottish during the privatisation of the Scottish Bus Group in August 1991, and at one time covered most of the Highlands, but sold out to Stagecoach in May 2008.

C635 KDS was a Volvo B10M-46/Caetano Algarve C49Ft that was purchased new by Park's of Hamilton in March 1986, and is shown arriving in Glasgow to operate a peak-hour express service to Strathaven. The firm traded as Park's Thistle Coaches from 1949 and were based in Strathaven. Operations later shifted to Hamilton and the company was refinanced in 1971 as Park's of Hamilton Limited, and continues to be one of Scotland's leading coach operators.

A32 UGA was a Bova EL28/581/Duple Calypso C57F that was purchased new by Henry Crawford of Neilston in January 1984. A total of fifty of the combination were bodied by Duple, and including the prototype, this made a grand total of fifty-one. Crawford's have been based at Shilford Mill near Uplawmoor since the 1970s and operate around two dozen coaches.

ULS 162X was a Volvo B58-61/Plaxton Supreme IV C53F that was delivered new to Fitzcharles of Grangemouth in January 1982. It was re-registered as 991 VRL in September 1983. The fleet was garaged at Newhouse Road in Grangemouth and around sixteen were in use at any time. Operations ceased in October 2015.

SYJ 948L was a Bedford YRQ/Plaxton Elite C45F that was purchased new by Watson's Tours of Dundee in January 1973. Watson's Tours was originally a family business, who built up a good coach tours operation based on Dundee. The fleet usually numbered around nine vehicles at any time. The company was taken over in 1973 by Thomas Meadows & Co. Ltd of London. They continued to operate as Watson's Tours and the fleet was increased to a dozen coaches, with Bedford as the chosen supplier. The business was purchased by Cotter's Tours of Glasgow in the 1980s.

VHV 109G was an AEC Reliance 6MU3R/Plaxton Elite C36C that was purchased new by Glenton Tours of London, SE14, in 1969. It was purchased by Clan Garage in 1976 and was upseated to C45C. They started an Isle of Skye to Glasgow express service, which ran under the 'Skyways' banner. VHV was photographed when resting at the company's depot in Kyle of Lochalsh.

HSD 712N was a Volvo B58-61/Alexander M Type C42Ft that was purchased new by Western SMT (V2541) in May 1975 for use on the Glasgow to London service. It passed to Black Prince of Morley in 1985 and was re-registered to 6571 WF. In 1987 it had joined the fleet of Globeheath of Bridgend, and two years later was purchased by McColl's Coaches. This view shows it at Auld Street depot in Dalmuir, just after McColl's had upseated it to C50F.